Leading with Impact: The First 50 Days

By MR. Raul Dominguez, MIO-PSYCH

Leading with Impact: The First 50 Days

Copyright © 2023 Raul Dominguez

All rights reserved.

ISBN: 9798397072403

All rights reserved. No part of this publication may be reproduced, distributed, or transmitted in any form or by any means, including photocopying, recording, or other electronic or mechanical methods, without the prior written permission of the publisher, except in the case of brief quotations embodied in critical reviews and certain other noncommercial uses permitted by copyright law. For permission requests, write to the publisher at the address below.

Mr. Raul Dominguez, MIO-Psych
Miami FL, USA

For the visionary leaders shaping a better tomorrow.

Content

BOOK SYNOPSIS: 6

CHAPTER 1: SETTING THE STAGE: PREPARING FOR LEADERSHIP TRANSITION 8

CHAPTER 2: DAY ONE: MAKING A STRONG FIRST IMPRESSION 12

CHAPTER 3: LEADING SELF: PERSONAL LEADERSHIP IN THE FIRST 50 DAYS 15

CHAPTER 4: BUILDING AND ALIGNING THE TEAM 20

CHAPTER 5: CREATING A CHANGE STRATEGY 24

CHAPTER 6: EXECUTING CHANGE: MOBILIZING THE ORGANIZATION 28

CHAPTER 7: LEADING WITH EMOTIONAL INTELLIGENCE..32

CHAPTER 8: ENGAGING AND INSPIRING THE ORGANIZATION 36

CHAPTER 9: NAVIGATING CHALLENGES AND OVERCOMING SETBACKS 39

CONCLUSION: REFLECTIONS ON THE FIRST 50 DAYS 43

LESSONS LEARNED AND KEY TAKEAWAYS...47

LOOKING AHEAD: SUSTAINING IMPACTFUL LEADERSHIP 51

Book Synopsis:

In "Leading with Impact: The First 50 Days," you will embark on a transformative journey to become an influential leader who drives meaningful change. Drawing upon comprehensive research and real-life experiences, this book provides a practical roadmap for newly appointed leaders in their critical first 50 days.

The book begins by emphasizing the importance of preparing for leadership transition. It explores how to assess the organization's landscape, craft a compelling leadership vision, and establish crucial relationships with key stakeholders.

Section I dives into establishing leadership foundations, starting with Day One. It unpacks the significance of making a strong first impression, setting the tone, and building trust and credibility with your team. The chapter on personal leadership highlights self-awareness, developing a resilient mindset, and mastering time management and prioritization.

Chapter 4 focuses on building and aligning the team, guiding leaders to assess their existing teams, develop a cohesive team culture, and align team members with the leadership vision.

Section II addresses driving impactful change within the organization. It presents a comprehensive approach to creating a change strategy, diagnosing the need for change, and developing a change roadmap. Leaders will learn how to effectively communicate change initiatives and gain buy-in from their teams.

Chapter 6 focuses on executing change by mobilizing the organization. Leaders will gain insights into change leadership and influencing skills, overcoming resistance and navigating obstacles, and effectively tracking progress and adjusting course.

Section III emphasizes sustaining momentum and growth. It explores leading with emotional intelligence, cultivating a positive and inclusive work environment, and empowering and developing others. Leaders will discover effective communication strategies, techniques to motivate and engage employees, and the importance of celebrating wins and recognizing achievements.

Chapter 9 delves into the inevitable challenges and setbacks leaders face, offering guidance on dealing with difficult situations, conflict resolution, learning from failures, and developing resilience and perseverance.

In the concluding chapter, the book reflects on the lessons learned and key takeaways from the first 50 days. It also provides a glimpse into the future, offering insights on how to sustain impactful leadership beyond the initial transition period.

"Leading with Impact: The First 50 Days" equips leaders with the tools, strategies, and mindset required to make a lasting impression, drive impactful change, and inspire teams to achieve greatness. This book will empower leaders to make a difference and leave a lasting legacy in their organizations.

Chapter 1: Setting the Stage: Preparing for Leadership Transition

Congratulations on your new leadership role! As you embark on this exciting journey, it is essential to lay a solid foundation for success. The first 50 days of your leadership are critical in establishing your presence, setting expectations, and building relationships. This chapter will guide you through the process of preparing for a seamless leadership transition, allowing you to hit the ground running and make a lasting impact.

1.1 Assessing the Landscape: Understanding the Organization

Imagine walking into a beautiful but unfamiliar garden. To truly appreciate its beauty and nurture its growth, you must take the time to understand its unique characteristics—the soil, climate, and the existing plants. Similarly, before diving into your new role, it is crucial to assess the organization you are stepping into.

Conduct a thorough assessment of its structure, culture, strengths, and areas for improvement. This goes beyond the superficial knowledge you may have gained during the hiring process. Dive deep into the organization's mission statement, values, and strategic objectives. Familiarize yourself with the company's history, its market position, and the industry landscape in which it operates.

Gaining insights into the organization's past and present will provide a comprehensive understanding of its identity and trajectory. Additionally, it will enable you to identify any potential challenges, opportunities, or blind spots that may exist. Consider conducting interviews or engaging in conversations with key stakeholders, such as executives, department heads, and long-term employees. Their perspectives will offer valuable insights into the organization's strengths, challenges, and opportunities.

Take the time to review financial reports, market analyses, and any available performance metrics. These documents will provide quantitative data that complements the qualitative understanding you have gathered. By combining these various sources of information, you will develop a comprehensive view of the organization's current state.

Through this assessment, you will identify the organization's unique culture, the dynamics between departments and teams, and any potential gaps that need to be addressed. This knowledge will serve as a solid foundation as you navigate the organization's dynamics and implement effective leadership strategies.

1.2 Crafting Your Leadership Vision: Defining Purpose and Goals

A ship without a destination is destined to drift aimlessly. As a leader, it is crucial to have a clear vision that inspires and guides your team. Take the time to reflect on your values, strengths, and aspirations. What do you want to achieve as a leader? What impact do you want to make on the organization and its stakeholders?

Crafting your leadership vision involves defining the purpose of your leadership and setting goals that align with the organization's mission and strategic objectives. Your vision should be inspiring and forward-thinking, motivating your team to strive for excellence.

Think of your vision as the North Star, guiding your actions and decisions. It should be ambitious yet achievable, providing a sense of direction and purpose. Consider involving key stakeholders and seeking their input when crafting your vision. This collaborative approach fosters a sense of ownership and commitment from the team, ensuring that the vision is aligned with their aspirations and the organization's overall goals.

Remember, a vision is not merely a set of words on paper–it should be lived and breathed by you and your team. As a leader, it is your responsibility to inspire others to embrace the vision and actively work towards its realization.

1.3 Building Relationships: Engaging with Key Stakeholders

Leadership is not a solitary journey–it is a collaborative effort. Effective leadership is built upon strong relationships with key stakeholders. These stakeholders include individuals and groups that have a vested interest in the success of the organization, such as executives, department heads, employees, customers, and partners.

Invest time in getting to know these stakeholders and understanding their roles, expectations, and concerns. Schedule one-on-one meetings or informal conversations to build rapport and establish open lines of communication. This will help you gain insights into the organization's dynamics, identify potential allies, and understand the perspectives of various stakeholders.

Building relationships also involves actively listening and demonstrating empathy. Show genuine interest in the opinions and experiences of others, fostering an environment of trust and collaboration. By actively engaging with key stakeholders, you create a network of support and leverage the collective wisdom and expertise within the organization.

In addition to internal stakeholders, consider reaching out to external stakeholders, such as industry leaders, partners, and community members. This broadens your perspective and allows you to build valuable connections beyond the organization's boundaries. These external relationships can provide insights, resources, and opportunities that can contribute to your success as a leader.

Remember that relationships are not built overnight. Building trust and establishing meaningful connections takes time and effort. Be patient, proactive, and authentic in your interactions. By investing in building strong relationships, you create a solid support system and foster a collaborative culture within the organization.

By proactively assessing the landscape, crafting your leadership vision, and building relationships, you will establish a solid foundation for your leadership transition. These initial steps will equip you with the knowledge, clarity, and support needed to make a powerful entrance into your new role.

As you move forward, Chapter 2 will explore the importance of making a strong first impression and setting the tone for your leadership journey. Get ready to make your mark in the first 24 hours as a leader and leave a lasting impression on your team and the organization.

Chapter 2: Day One: Making a Strong First Impression

2.1 The Power of First Impressions

They say you only get one chance to make a first impression, and as a leader, that chance is amplified. The first day in your new role sets the tone for your entire leadership journey. It is an opportunity to make a lasting impact and establish yourself as a confident and capable leader. Understand that your actions, words, and demeanor during this crucial period will be closely observed by your team and stakeholders. The power of a positive first impression cannot be underestimated.

Think about the last time you met someone new. What were your initial impressions? The way you carry yourself, the way you speak, and the way you engage with others all contribute to the perception people form about you. This is equally true in a leadership role. Your team members will be looking to you for guidance, inspiration, and reassurance. By making a positive first impression, you set the stage for building trust, credibility, and a strong foundation for your leadership.

2.2 Setting the Tone: Communicating Expectations

On your first day, it is important to communicate your expectations clearly. Your team is eager to understand how your leadership will shape their work and the organization as a whole. Take the time to articulate your expectations regarding performance, collaboration, and values. Set the tone for a culture of excellence, accountability, and open communication. By clearly expressing your expectations, you provide a framework for your team to understand what is required of them and how their efforts contribute to the organization's success.

Consider the example of a newly appointed CEO entering a company known for its innovative culture. On their first day, they gather the entire organization for a town hall meeting. In this meeting, they emphasize their commitment to fostering creativity and encourage employees to think outside the box. By clearly communicating this expectation from day one, the CEO sets the tone for a culture that values and rewards innovative thinking. This inspires employees to bring their best ideas forward and contribute to the organization's growth and success.

In addition to communicating expectations verbally, it is crucial to lead by example. Your actions speak louder than words. Demonstrate the behavior and mindset you expect from your team. If you value transparency and open communication, model these behaviors by actively seeking input, sharing information, and providing regular feedback. By setting the tone through your own actions, you create a sense of alignment and inspire your team to follow suit.

2.3 Building Trust and Credibility

Trust is the cornerstone of effective leadership. During your first 50 days, focus on building trust and credibility with your team. Be authentic and approachable, demonstrating your willingness to listen and learn. Act with integrity and follow through on your commitments. Trust is earned through consistent actions and transparent communication.

Consider the scenario of a manager stepping into a team that has experienced a high turnover rate and low morale. To build trust, the manager takes the time to meet with each team member individually, actively listening to their concerns and challenges. They address these concerns openly and honestly, laying out their plans to support the team and create a positive work environment. By being authentic and responsive, the manager begins to rebuild trust, showing the team that they are committed to their success and well-being.

Invest time in getting to know your team members individually, their strengths, and their challenges. Show empathy and offer support where needed. By building genuine connections and demonstrating your genuine interest in their well-being and success, you will establish a culture of trust and create a strong foundation for collaboration.

Remember that the first 24 hours as a leader are a critical window of opportunity. By making a strong first impression, setting clear expectations, and building trust, you lay the groundwork for a successful leadership journey.

As you move forward, Chapter 3 will focus on leading yourself, highlighting the importance of self-awareness, developing a leadership mindset, and effective time management in the first 50 days of your leadership role. Get ready to unleash your full potential and lead with impact from within.

Chapter 3: Leading Self: Personal Leadership in the First 50 Days

Leadership begins with self-leadership. In order to effectively lead others, it is essential to first understand and lead oneself. Chapter 3 will explore the crucial aspects of personal leadership during the first 50 days of your leadership role. By focusing on self-awareness, developing a leadership mindset, and mastering time management, you will enhance your effectiveness as a leader and set the stage for long-term success.

3.1 Self-Awareness: Understanding Strengths and Weaknesses

Self-awareness is the foundation of personal leadership. It involves having a deep understanding of your strengths, weaknesses, values, and aspirations. The first 50 days provide a valuable opportunity to reflect on your own capabilities and areas for growth.

Take the time to assess your leadership style and preferences. Consider seeking feedback from trusted mentors, colleagues, or even your team members. This feedback can provide valuable insights into your leadership strengths and areas where you may need to develop further. Embrace constructive criticism and use it as a catalyst for personal growth.

By understanding your strengths, you can leverage them to inspire and motivate others. For example, if you excel in strategic thinking, you can use this strength to guide your team in setting and achieving long-term goals. On the other hand, identifying your weaknesses allows you to proactively address them. Seek opportunities for learning and development in areas where you may need improvement, whether it's communication, decision-making, or emotional intelligence.

Self-awareness also extends to recognizing your values and aligning them with your leadership approach. Reflect on what is truly important to you as a leader. Is it integrity, empathy, or innovation? By leading in alignment with your values, you create a sense of authenticity and build trust with your team.

3.2 Developing Leadership Mindset and Resilience

A leadership mindset is the lens through which you perceive and respond to challenges and opportunities. It shapes your beliefs, attitudes, and behaviors as a leader. Cultivating a growth mindset is essential for navigating the complexities of leadership.

Embrace the belief that challenges are opportunities for growth and learning. Emphasize a solutions-oriented approach, focusing on finding creative and innovative ways to overcome obstacles. Develop a mindset that welcomes feedback and views failure as a stepping stone toward improvement.

Resilience is a key attribute of effective leaders. The ability to bounce back from setbacks, adapt to change, and maintain a positive attitude in the face of adversity is crucial. During the first 50 days, you may encounter unexpected challenges or resistance to change. It is important to remain resilient and inspire your team to do the same.

To build resilience, engage in self-care practices that nurture your physical, mental, and emotional well-being. This includes exercise, meditation, setting boundaries, and seeking support from mentors or coaches. Prioritize self-care to maintain your energy, focus, and overall well-being as a leader.

3.3 Time Management and Prioritization

As a leader, your time is a valuable resource. Effectively managing your time is essential for accomplishing your goals, driving initiatives forward, and ensuring that you are available for your team when they need you.

Start by assessing your current time management practices. Identify any inefficiencies or time-consuming tasks that can be delegated or eliminated. Prioritize your responsibilities based on their importance and urgency. Develop a clear understanding of your most critical objectives and allocate your time accordingly.

Consider implementing time management techniques such as prioritizing tasks using the Eisenhower Matrix, setting clear boundaries and time blocks for focused work, and leveraging technology tools for efficient scheduling and task management.

Delegate tasks that can be effectively handled by others, empowering your team members and freeing up your time for higher-level strategic activities. Effective delegation not only allows you to manage your workload but also fosters growth and development within your team.

Remember, effective time management is not just about being busy but about being productive. By mastering time management and prioritization, you can maximize your impact as a leader and create a culture of productivity within your team.

Leading yourself is the first step toward leading others with impact. By cultivating self-awareness, developing a leadership mindset, and mastering time management, you set the foundation for effective leadership in the first 50 days and beyond. As you embark on this journey of self-leadership, you will not only enhance your own capabilities but also inspire and empower those around you. In Chapter 4, we will delve into building and aligning the team, exploring strategies for assessing the existing team, fostering a cohesive team culture, and aligning the team with your leadership vision. Get ready to unleash the collective potential of your team and drive impactful results.

Here are a few examples to support the theories discussed in Chapter 3:

1. **Self-Awareness: Understanding Strengths and Weaknesses**

Example 1: Sarah, a newly appointed manager, discovers through self-reflection and feedback from her team that she excels in strategic thinking and problem-solving. Recognizing this strength, she leverages it by involving her team in collaborative decision-making processes, encouraging them to contribute their ideas and perspectives. This not only empowers her team members but also leads to innovative solutions and increased engagement.

Example 2: John, a leader in a fast-paced startup, identifies through self-awareness that his communication skills need improvement. He takes proactive steps to address this weakness by attending communication workshops, seeking guidance from mentors, and practicing active listening. As a result, his team experiences clearer communication, better alignment, and improved collaboration.

2. **Developing Leadership Mindset and Resilience**

Example 1: Lisa, a CEO facing a major industry disruption, embraces a growth mindset and encourages her team to do the same. Instead of viewing the disruption as a threat, they see it as an opportunity for innovation and growth. They experiment with new business models, pivot their strategies, and adapt to the changing landscape. Through their resilience and growth mindset, they navigate the challenges and emerge stronger, maintaining their market position and expanding their customer base.

Example 2: Mark, a team leader, faces a setback when a major project fails to meet its objectives. Instead of dwelling on the failure, he adopts a positive mindset and encourages his team to focus on the lessons learned. They conduct a thorough analysis of the project, identify areas for improvement, and implement changes in their approach. By embracing a resilient mindset, Mark and his team bounce back, delivering successful projects in the future and fostering a culture of continuous learning.

3. **Time Management and Prioritization**

Example 1: Emily, a senior manager, realizes that she often gets overwhelmed with administrative tasks and finds it challenging to focus on strategic initiatives. To address this, she delegates routine administrative tasks to her team members, empowering them to take ownership and freeing up her time for high-level decision-making and strategic planning. This shift allows Emily to allocate her time more effectively and drive impactful outcomes for the organization.

Example 2: Alex, a project manager, uses time management techniques to prioritize tasks and meet project deadlines. He applies the Eisenhower Matrix to categorize tasks based on their urgency and importance. By focusing on high-priority tasks and delegating or eliminating non-essential ones, Alex ensures that his team remains focused on critical project deliverables, resulting in successful project completion within the given timeframe.

These examples demonstrate how self-awareness, a leadership mindset, and effective time management can positively impact leaders and their teams, leading to enhanced performance, growth, and resilience in the face of challenges.

Chapter 4: Building and Aligning the Team

Leading a high-performing team is essential for achieving organizational goals and driving impactful results. In Chapter 4, we will explore the critical aspects of building and aligning the team during the first 50 days of your leadership role. By assessing the existing team, developing a cohesive team culture, and aligning the team with your leadership vision, you will create a strong and unified foundation for success.

4.1 Assessing the Existing Team

Before making any changes or implementing new strategies, it is crucial to assess the strengths, weaknesses, and dynamics of the existing team. Take the time to understand the composition of the team, their individual skills and expertise, and how they work together.

Conduct one-on-one meetings with team members to gain insights into their aspirations, challenges, and areas where they feel they can contribute more. This open and honest dialogue allows you to identify opportunities for growth, address any underlying issues, and align individual goals with the overall team objectives.

Consider using assessment tools, such as personality assessments or 360-degree feedback, to gather additional information about the team's dynamics and areas for development. This data provides valuable insights into individual strengths, areas of improvement, and potential skill gaps that need to be addressed.

Example:

During his first 50 days as a team leader, Alex conducts individual meetings with each team member to assess their skills, strengths, and areas for development. Through these conversations, he discovers that Sarah, a team member, possesses excellent analytical skills that have been underutilized. Alex takes this opportunity to assign Sarah to a challenging project that aligns with her skills, providing her with an opportunity to shine and contribute significantly to the team's success. By assessing the existing team, Alex is able to leverage their talents effectively, leading to increased motivation and productivity.

4.2 Developing a Cohesive Team Culture

A cohesive team culture is built on trust, collaboration, and shared values. As a leader, it is your responsibility to foster an environment where team members feel safe to express their opinions, support one another, and work toward common goals.

Communicate the team's purpose and align it with the organization's mission and vision. Clearly articulate the values and expectations that define the team's culture. Encourage open and transparent communication, active listening, and constructive feedback among team members.

Promote a sense of psychological safety, where team members feel comfortable taking risks, sharing ideas, and learning from failures. Celebrate diversity and encourage inclusive practices, ensuring that every team member feels valued and respected for their unique contributions.

Example:

Natalie, a newly appointed team leader, recognizes the importance of developing a cohesive team culture. She organizes team-building activities, such as off-site retreats and team lunches, to foster camaraderie and build trust among team members. Additionally, she creates a shared team charter that outlines the team's values, expectations, and commitments. By promoting a culture of collaboration and inclusivity, Natalie creates a supportive environment where team members feel empowered to share their ideas and contribute to the team's success.

4.3 Aligning the Team with the Leadership Vision

To drive impactful results, it is essential to align the team's goals and objectives with your leadership vision. Clearly communicate your vision to the team, highlighting how their individual contributions fit into the bigger picture. Help team members understand how their work directly impacts the organization's mission and the value they bring to the table.

Provide a sense of direction by setting clear goals, both short-term and long-term, that align with the vision. Break down these goals into actionable steps and involve the team in the goal-setting process. This fosters a sense of ownership and commitment among team members, motivating them to strive for excellence.

Example:

Daniel, a leader in a technology company, shares his vision of becoming a market leader in innovative solutions with his team. He conducts regular team meetings to discuss the progress towards this vision, shares success stories, and recognizes individual contributions. Daniel sets SMART goals with his team, ensuring they are specific, measurable, attainable, relevant, and time-bound. By aligning the team's objectives with his leadership vision, Daniel creates a sense of purpose and motivation, driving the team towards achieving their collective goals.

Building and aligning the team is a critical aspect of leadership in the first 50 days and beyond. By assessing the existing team, developing a cohesive team culture, and aligning the team with your leadership vision, you create a solid foundation for collaboration, innovation, and success. In Chapter 5, we will explore strategies for creating a change strategy, diagnosing the need for change, and gaining buy-in for change initiatives. Get ready to drive impactful change and propel your team towards greater achievements.

Chapter 5: Creating a Change Strategy

In today's dynamic and competitive business landscape, change is not only necessary but inevitable for organizations to thrive. In Chapter 5, we will delve into the intricacies of creating a change strategy during the first 50 days of your leadership role. By diagnosing the need for change, developing a comprehensive change roadmap, and effectively communicating and gaining buy-in for change initiatives, you will pave the way for a successful and impactful transformation.

5.1 Diagnosing the Need for Change

Diagnosing the need for change is the crucial first step in creating a change strategy. It involves understanding the current state of the organization, identifying areas that require improvement or adaptation, and uncovering the underlying factors driving the need for change.

One effective approach to diagnose the need for change is by conducting a SWOT analysis (Strengths, Weaknesses, Opportunities, and Threats). This analysis allows you to assess the internal strengths and weaknesses of the organization, as well as the external opportunities and threats it faces. By identifying these factors, you gain insights into areas that require transformation and potential avenues for growth.

Another useful diagnostic tool is the Kotter's 8-Step Change Model, which emphasizes the importance of urgency, creating a guiding coalition, and developing a shared vision for change. By applying this model, you can pinpoint areas within the organization where change is most needed and develop a solid foundation for your change strategy.

Example:

Rebecca, a newly appointed HR director, diagnoses the need for change within her organization through a combination of approaches. She conducts employee surveys and focus groups to gather feedback on pain points and areas of improvement. The feedback highlights a lack of employee engagement, outdated performance management systems, and a need for better work-life balance initiatives. By diagnosing these needs, Rebecca realizes the importance of implementing a comprehensive employee engagement program, updating performance management practices, and introducing flexible work arrangements to enhance productivity and employee satisfaction.

5.2 Developing a Change Roadmap

Once you have diagnosed the need for change, the next step is to develop a well-defined change roadmap that outlines the specific steps, resources, and timelines required to achieve your desired outcomes. A change roadmap provides a clear direction for the organization and helps manage expectations throughout the change process.

Start by setting SMART goals (Specific, Measurable, Achievable, Relevant, and Time-bound) that align with the overall vision and objectives of the organization. Break down these goals into smaller milestones or initiatives that are more manageable and actionable. This enables you to track progress, celebrate achievements, and make necessary adjustments along the way.

Allocate resources strategically, including budget, personnel, and technology, to support the change initiatives outlined in the roadmap. Identify any potential risks or barriers that may impede the success of the change efforts, and develop contingency plans to mitigate these risks.

Example:

Mark, a senior operations manager, develops a change roadmap to address a decline in operational efficiency within his department. His change roadmap includes the goal of reducing turnaround time by 20% within six months. To achieve this goal, Mark identifies initiatives such as process optimization, employee training programs, and the implementation of new technologies. By breaking down the roadmap into specific initiatives with clear timelines and resource allocations, Mark ensures a structured and focused approach to achieving the desired outcomes.

5.3 Communicating and Gaining Buy-in for Change Initiatives

Effective communication and gaining buy-in from stakeholders are crucial elements of successful change management. Engaging and involving key stakeholders, including employees, senior leaders, and external partners, ensures their understanding, commitment, and support for the change initiatives.

Develop a comprehensive communication plan that outlines the key messages, channels, and frequency of communication. Tailor your messages to resonate with different stakeholder groups and address their specific concerns or expectations. Transparency is key during this stage, as it builds trust and cultivates a sense of shared purpose.

Create opportunities for dialogue and feedback to encourage two-way communication. This allows stakeholders to express their thoughts, concerns, and ideas, while also providing you with valuable insights and perspectives. Address any resistance or misconceptions promptly, and provide clarity on the roles and responsibilities of stakeholders during the change process.

Example:

Emily, a change leader, undertakes a robust communication strategy to gain buy-in for a digital transformation initiative within her organization. She conducts town hall meetings, departmental workshops, and one-on-one sessions to communicate the vision and rationale behind the change. Emily also leverages various communication channels, such as intranet portals, newsletters, and social media platforms, to provide regular updates and success stories related to the ongoing transformation. By engaging stakeholders through multiple channels and facilitating open communication, Emily fosters a culture of collaboration and support for the change initiative.

Creating a change strategy is a critical step in leading impactful change within your organization. By diagnosing the need for change, developing a comprehensive change roadmap, and effectively communicating and gaining buy-in for change initiatives, you establish a strong foundation for successful transformation. In Chapter 6, we will delve into executing change, focusing on mobilizing the organization, overcoming resistance, and tracking progress. Get ready to drive and implement impactful change initiatives that will propel your organization toward greater success.

Chapter 6: Executing Change: Mobilizing the Organization

Now that you have developed a solid change strategy, it is time to shift your focus to executing the change and mobilizing your organization. Chapter 6 will explore the key aspects of leading change during the first 50 days of your leadership role. We will delve into change leadership and influencing skills, overcoming resistance and navigating obstacles, and tracking progress and adjusting course along the way. By mastering these strategies, you will effectively drive and execute impactful change initiatives that propel your organization forward.

6.1 Change Leadership and Influencing Skills

Change leadership requires a unique set of skills to inspire and guide your team through the transformation process. Effective change leaders understand the importance of communication, empathy, and influence in gaining support and buy-in from stakeholders at all levels of the organization.

Developing strong influencing skills enables you to articulate the benefits of the change, address concerns, and motivate others to embrace new ways of working. This involves crafting persuasive messages, building relationships based on trust and credibility, and adapting your communication style to resonate with different individuals and groups.

As a change leader, it is essential to communicate the vision and purpose of the change clearly. By painting a compelling picture of the future state and highlighting the benefits it brings, you can ignite enthusiasm and garner support from your team and other stakeholders. Use storytelling techniques, visuals, and real-life examples to make the vision relatable and inspiring.

Building strong relationships based on trust and credibility is another crucial aspect of change leadership. Take the time to connect with individuals, listen to their concerns, and understand their perspectives. By demonstrating empathy and genuine interest in their well-being, you create a supportive environment where people are more willing to embrace change.

Example:

Sarah, a change leader in a manufacturing company, demonstrates excellent change leadership and influencing skills during a major process improvement initiative. She holds regular meetings with key stakeholders, including production managers and frontline employees, to explain the benefits of the proposed changes and address their concerns. Sarah actively listens to their feedback, incorporates their ideas into the implementation plan, and celebrates their contributions. By leveraging her influencing skills, Sarah gains the support and commitment of the entire team, resulting in a successful implementation of the new process.

6.2 Overcoming Resistance and Navigating Obstacles

Resistance to change is a common challenge that leaders encounter during the execution phase. Overcoming resistance requires a proactive and empathetic approach to address the concerns and fears of individuals or groups affected by the change.

Start by understanding the reasons behind the resistance. Is it due to fear of the unknown, loss of control, or concerns about personal impact? By identifying the root causes of resistance, you can tailor your communication and change management strategies to address these specific concerns.

Engage in open and honest dialogue, actively listen to the perspectives of those resisting the change, and provide clear and transparent explanations about the rationale and benefits of the change. Offer support, training, and resources to help individuals adapt to new processes or ways of working. Create a safe and inclusive environment where individuals feel comfortable expressing their concerns and actively participating in the change process.

As a change leader, it is crucial to be resilient in the face of resistance. Expect challenges and setbacks along the way, and be prepared to handle them with a positive mindset. Foster a culture of continuous learning and improvement, where mistakes are seen as opportunities for growth. Encourage experimentation and innovation, and celebrate small wins to build momentum and overcome resistance.

Example:

John, a project manager leading a software implementation, faces resistance from a group of employees who are apprehensive about learning new technology. To navigate this obstacle, John organizes training sessions and workshops to address their concerns and build their confidence. He also assigns change champions within the team who can provide additional support and serve as role models. By addressing the resistance head-on and providing the necessary resources and support, John successfully guides the team through the change, resulting in increased productivity and efficiency.

6.3 Tracking Progress and Adjusting Course

Change is a dynamic process that requires continuous monitoring and adjustment. Tracking the progress of change initiatives allows you to identify any gaps or deviations from the desired outcomes and make timely adjustments to ensure success.

Establish key performance indicators (KPIs) and milestones to measure the progress of the change initiatives. Regularly assess and evaluate the data to identify areas of improvement or potential barriers. Encourage feedback from stakeholders and use it to fine-tune your strategies and address any emerging challenges.

Flexibility and adaptability are essential during the execution phase. Be open to revising your plans, reallocating resources, or exploring alternative approaches if needed. Communicate these adjustments clearly to stakeholders and ensure they understand the rationale behind the changes.

Example:

Michelle, a change agent leading a cultural transformation initiative, sets specific KPIs to track the progress of the change. She regularly collects feedback through surveys, focus groups, and individual interviews to gather insights from employees. Based on the data collected, Michelle identifies areas where the desired outcomes are not being achieved and adjusts the change strategies accordingly. She communicates the adjustments to the team, highlighting the reasons behind the changes and the expected benefits. Through continuous monitoring and adjustment, Michelle ensures the successful execution of the cultural transformation, resulting in improved employee engagement and collaboration.

Executing change and mobilizing the organization is a critical phase in the first 50 days of your leadership role. By leveraging change leadership and influencing skills, overcoming resistance, and navigating obstacles, and tracking progress while adjusting course, you will drive impactful change initiatives that propel your organization toward success. In Chapter 7, we will explore the importance of leading with emotional intelligence and cultivating a positive and inclusive work environment. Get ready to empower and develop others as you continue your journey of impactful leadership.

Chapter 7: Leading with Emotional Intelligence

In today's rapidly changing and complex business landscape, effective leaders must go beyond technical skills and tap into the power of emotional intelligence to inspire, motivate, and guide their teams. Chapter 7 dives deep into the importance of leading with emotional intelligence in the crucial first 50 days of your leadership role. We will explore the key aspects of cultivating emotional intelligence as a leader, fostering a positive and inclusive work environment, and empowering and developing others. By harnessing the full potential of emotional intelligence, you will create a thriving and high-performing organization.

7.1 Cultivating Emotional Intelligence as a Leader

Emotional intelligence (EI) is the ability to recognize, understand, and manage our own emotions, as well as effectively perceive and navigate the emotions of others. Cultivating emotional intelligence allows leaders to build stronger relationships, make better decisions, and create a positive work environment.

Start by developing self-awareness, the foundation of emotional intelligence. Take the time to reflect on your own emotions, triggers, and patterns of behavior. Understand your strengths and weaknesses, as well as the impact your emotions have on those around you. By becoming more self-aware, you can respond to challenging situations with greater emotional intelligence.

Emotional self-regulation is another crucial aspect of emotional intelligence. It involves managing your emotions and impulses in a way that allows you to think and act in a balanced and constructive manner. Practice techniques such as deep breathing, mindfulness, and self-reflection to cultivate emotional self-regulation and enhance your leadership effectiveness.

Example:

Jennifer, a senior executive, demonstrates exceptional emotional intelligence in her leadership style. She prioritizes self-awareness by regularly engaging in self-reflection and seeking feedback from her team. Jennifer acknowledges her own emotions and understands their potential impact on decision-making. In high-pressure situations, she takes a moment to breathe and reflect, allowing herself to respond thoughtfully rather than react impulsively. This level of emotional self-regulation fosters an environment of composure and confidence among her team members.

7.2 Fostering a Positive and Inclusive Work Environment

A positive and inclusive work environment is essential for employee engagement, collaboration, and overall organizational success. As a leader, you have the power to create and nurture such an environment through your actions and behaviors.

Start by demonstrating empathy and compassion towards your team members. Take the time to listen actively and show genuine interest in their well-being. By understanding their needs and concerns, you can build trust and establish stronger connections. Acknowledge their accomplishments, provide constructive feedback, and offer support when needed. By creating a sense of psychological safety, you encourage open communication and foster trust among team members.

Promote diversity and inclusion within your organization. Recognize and value the unique perspectives and contributions of individuals from different backgrounds and experiences. Encourage collaboration and create opportunities for diverse voices to be heard. Embrace inclusive leadership practices, such as seeking diverse opinions, mitigating biases, and fostering a culture of belonging.

Example:

David, a team leader in a technology startup, is known for fostering a positive and inclusive work environment. He actively listens to his team members, ensuring that their opinions are heard and respected. David encourages a culture of collaboration by organizing regular brainstorming sessions and team-building activities. He celebrates diversity by promoting cross-functional teams, allowing employees from different departments to work together and share their expertise. This inclusive approach creates a sense of belonging and enhances overall team performance.

7.3 Empowering and Developing Others

As a leader, one of your primary responsibilities is to empower and develop your team members. By providing them with the necessary support, resources, and opportunities for growth, you cultivate a high-performance culture and unleash their full potential.

Delegate responsibilities and empower your team members to make decisions and take ownership of their work. Provide them with clear expectations, autonomy, and the necessary tools to succeed. Offer guidance and mentorship, and create a culture of continuous learning and development.

Recognize and celebrate the achievements of your team members. Provide constructive feedback and opportunities for growth, both through formal performance evaluations and informal coaching conversations. Encourage them to stretch their capabilities and take on new challenges, fostering a culture of innovation and personal development.

Example:

Lisa, a project manager, excels in empowering and developing her team members. She delegates tasks based on individual strengths and interests, allowing team members to take ownership of their work. Lisa provides ongoing feedback and support, helping them identify areas for improvement and providing guidance for their professional development. She also encourages them to attend relevant workshops and training programs to enhance their skills. As a result of Lisa's efforts, her team members feel valued and empowered, leading to higher levels of engagement and productivity.

Leading with emotional intelligence is a powerful tool for driving organizational success. By cultivating emotional intelligence as a leader, fostering a positive and inclusive work environment, and empowering and developing others, you create a culture of trust, collaboration, and growth. In Chapter 8, we will explore effective communication strategies to engage and inspire your organization. Get ready to enhance your communication skills and motivate your team towards shared goals.

Chapter 8: Engaging and Inspiring the Organization

In Chapter 8, we explore the crucial aspect of engaging and inspiring the organization. Effective leaders understand that engagement is not just a buzzword; it is the key to unlocking the full potential of their team members and driving exceptional performance. In this chapter, we delve into the strategies and techniques that will enable you to communicate effectively, motivate your employees, and create a work environment that fosters engagement, collaboration, and innovation.

8.1: Effective Communication Strategies

The Power of Communication: Communication is the lifeblood of leadership. We discuss the importance of clear and open communication, active listening, and the art of giving and receiving feedback. Through practical examples and actionable tips, we help you develop the skills to communicate effectively and foster a culture of transparent and constructive dialogue.

Tailoring Your Message: We explore the significance of adapting your communication style to different individuals and situations. Understanding the diverse perspectives, needs, and preferences of your team members allows you to deliver your message with maximum impact, ensuring that it resonates with each person in your organization.

Overcoming Communication Barriers: We address common communication challenges, such as language barriers, remote work settings, and cultural differences. By providing strategies to overcome these obstacles, you will be equipped to foster effective communication across all levels of your organization.

8.2: Motivating and Engaging Employees

Understanding Motivation: Motivated employees are the driving force behind organizational success. We explore various motivation theories and discuss how you can leverage them to inspire and energize your team. By understanding what drives individuals, you can tailor your leadership approach and create an environment where everyone feels valued and motivated to perform at their best.

Empowering Through Autonomy: We emphasize the importance of empowering your employees by granting them autonomy and decision-making authority. We delve into the benefits of autonomy, share practical techniques for delegating effectively, and discuss how to balance autonomy with accountability to foster a culture of ownership and empowerment.

Recognition and Rewards: Recognition and rewards play a vital role in boosting employee morale and engagement. We explore different methods of recognizing and appreciating your team members' contributions, including both monetary and non-monetary incentives. By implementing effective recognition strategies, you will foster a positive and fulfilling work environment where employees feel valued and motivated.

8.3: Celebrating Wins and Recognizing Achievements

The Importance of Celebration: Celebrating wins and recognizing achievements not only boosts morale but also reinforces a culture of success and continuous improvement. We discuss the significance of celebrating milestones, both big and small, and provide ideas and best practices for creating a culture of celebration within your team.

Creating Meaningful Recognition Programs: We delve into the design and implementation of recognition programs that go beyond superficial gestures. We explore the power of personalized recognition, peer-to-peer recognition, and creating a sense of purpose and meaning behind the recognition efforts.

Inspiring Through Vision and Purpose: Finally, we emphasize the importance of inspiring your team by aligning their work with a compelling vision and purpose. We discuss how to articulate and communicate a compelling vision that resonates with your employees' values and aspirations, igniting their passion and commitment to achieving shared goals.

Chapter 8 concludes with a reminder of the critical role effective communication, motivation, and recognition play in engaging and inspiring the organization. By employing the strategies and techniques outlined in this chapter, you will foster a culture of engagement, collaboration, and high performance, creating an environment where individuals are inspired to bring their best selves to work every day. With engaged and motivated employees, you will not only achieve remarkable results but also cultivate a workplace where people thrive and find fulfillment in their work.

Chapter 9: Navigating Challenges and Overcoming Setbacks

Leadership is not without its challenges and setbacks. In Chapter 9, we delve into the art of navigating through difficult situations, managing conflicts, learning from failures, and cultivating resilience and perseverance. By mastering these skills, you will emerge as a stronger and more effective leader, capable of guiding your team through adversity and achieving long-term success.

9.1 Dealing with Difficult Situations and Conflict

Difficult situations and conflicts are inevitable in any leadership role. The key is to approach them with a strategic and empathetic mindset, seeking resolution and fostering collaboration.

First, embrace open communication. Create a safe space where team members can express their concerns, share differing viewpoints, and engage in constructive dialogue. Actively listen to all parties involved and strive to understand their perspectives. By demonstrating empathy and promoting open communication, you can de-escalate conflicts and find mutually beneficial solutions.

Next, employ effective conflict resolution techniques. Encourage compromise and find common ground among conflicting parties. Mediate and facilitate discussions to ensure that everyone's voice is heard and that a fair resolution is reached. Maintain a focus on the team's goals and values, keeping the bigger picture in mind.

Example:

John, a team leader in a marketing agency, encounters a conflict between two team members who have differing opinions on a crucial project. Instead of ignoring the conflict, John initiates a conversation with each team member individually to understand their concerns. He then brings them together for a collaborative discussion, guiding them towards finding a compromise that aligns with the project objectives. By fostering open communication and effective conflict resolution, John successfully resolves the conflict and restores harmony within the team.

9.2 Learning from Failures and Adapting to Change

Failures and setbacks are inevitable in any leadership journey. However, the key to success lies in how leaders respond and learn from these experiences. Embrace failures as opportunities for growth and personal development.

First, foster a culture of psychological safety within your team. Create an environment where mistakes are viewed as learning opportunities, not sources of blame or judgment. Encourage team members to share their failures openly, and lead by example by sharing your own experiences and lessons learned.

Next, practice reflective thinking. Analyze the factors that contributed to the failure and identify areas for improvement. Encourage your team to do the same, facilitating discussions on lessons learned and potential solutions. Emphasize the importance of continuous improvement and adaptability in the face of change.

Example:

Sarah, a project manager, encounters a project setback due to unforeseen circumstances. Instead of dwelling on the failure, she gathers her team for a reflective session. They collectively analyze the factors that led to the setback, identify areas for improvement, and brainstorm potential solutions. By encouraging open dialogue and a growth mindset, Sarah transforms the failure into a valuable learning experience. The team emerges stronger and more resilient, ready to tackle future challenges.

9.3 Resilience and Perseverance in Leadership

Resilience is the ability to bounce back from adversity, setbacks, and challenges. As a leader, it is crucial to cultivate resilience within yourself and inspire it in others.

Build your own resilience by maintaining a positive mindset and focusing on solutions rather than dwelling on problems. Embrace a growth mindset, recognizing that setbacks are temporary and can be overcome with perseverance. Take care of your physical and mental well-being, as they are essential for maintaining resilience during challenging times.

Additionally, support the resilience of your team members. Acknowledge their efforts and provide encouragement and support during difficult periods. Foster a culture of teamwork and collaboration, where team members can lean on each other for support and share the load during challenging times. Celebrate successes and milestones, boosting morale and motivation.

Example:

Mark, a CEO of a tech startup, faces a significant setback when a major investor unexpectedly pulls out of a funding round. Despite the setback, Mark maintains a positive mindset and rallies his team. He shares his vision for the company's future, reiterating their collective purpose and the value they bring to their customers. Mark encourages open communication and supports team members in exploring alternative funding options. Through his resilience and perseverance, Mark inspires his team to remain focused and motivated, ultimately securing new investors and propelling the company forward.

In Chapter 9, we explored the importance of navigating challenges and overcoming setbacks as a leader. By dealing with difficult situations and conflict, learning from failures, and cultivating resilience and perseverance, you will emerge as a resilient leader capable of guiding your team through adversity. In the final chapter, we reflect on the lessons learned from the first 50 days of leadership and explore strategies for sustaining impactful leadership in the long run. Get ready to embrace the future and lead with lasting impact.

Conclusion: Reflections on the First 50 Days

As we reach the conclusion of our exploration into the first 50 days of leadership, it is essential to take a moment to reflect on the profound insights gained, the transformative growth experienced, and the significant impact made. This critical period of leadership transition has laid the groundwork for your entire tenure, shaping your approach, and setting the stage for future success. By immersing ourselves in the principles and strategies outlined in this book, we have equipped ourselves with the tools and wisdom necessary to lead with unparalleled impact and effect positive change within our organizations.

Throughout this captivating journey, we embarked on a multifaceted exploration of the key components that contribute to a successful leadership transition. We embarked on our quest by diligently preparing ourselves for the role, meticulously assessing the complex landscape of our organizations, discerning the intricate nuances that shape its culture and operations. This foundational step allowed us to chart our course and craft a compelling leadership vision that embodies purpose and fosters alignment with the organization's overarching goals.

Our voyage further navigated towards the importance of building and nurturing relationships with key stakeholders. By engaging in genuine and meaningful connections, we cultivated alliances and partnerships that form the bedrock of effective leadership. These connections, grounded in trust, communication, and empathy, served as conduits for collaboration, synergy, and shared success.

Section I delved deep into the process of establishing leadership foundations, starting with the critical endeavor of making a strong first impression. Recognizing the power of first impressions, we harnessed our presence, charisma, and ability to inspire confidence, setting the tone for our leadership tenure. We strategically communicated expectations, creating a clear roadmap that guided our teams towards shared goals and facilitated effective performance.

But leadership begins within ourselves. Chapter 3 illuminated the significance of leading self, emphasizing the vital role of self-awareness in understanding our strengths and weaknesses. Armed with this knowledge, we cultivated a leadership mindset, honing our resilience and fortitude to weather any storm that may come our way. We mastered the art of time management and prioritization, skillfully balancing our commitments and responsibilities to optimize productivity and focus on the most critical tasks.

No leader stands alone; the strength of a team lies at the heart of every successful enterprise. Chapter 4 unveiled the secrets to building and aligning teams, starting with a comprehensive assessment of existing team dynamics. By understanding the unique composition, strengths, and areas for improvement within our teams, we curated an environment conducive to growth, collaboration, and innovation. We fostered a cohesive team culture, cultivating trust, respect, and open communication, while ensuring alignment with our overarching leadership vision.

Section II propelled us into the realm of driving impactful change, beginning with the art of creating a change strategy. We honed our diagnostic skills, adeptly identifying the need for change and crafting comprehensive roadmaps to guide our organizations through transformation. Effectively communicating these change initiatives and garnering buy-in from stakeholders became our guiding light, inspiring the entire organization to embrace change and actively contribute to its successful execution.

Chapter 6 propelled us further into the realm of executing change, honing our change leadership and influencing skills to mobilize the organization. We fearlessly confronted resistance and navigated obstacles that arose along the way, using our ingenuity and determination to transform challenges into opportunities. By meticulously tracking progress and nimbly adjusting our course, we ensured the sustained momentum and success of our change initiatives.

Section III immersed us in the transformative power of emotional intelligence. Chapter 7 illuminated the criticality of cultivating emotional intelligence as a leader, harnessing the power of empathy, self-regulation, and social skills. We fostered a positive and inclusive work environment, nurturing a sense of belonging and psychological safety that unleashed the full potential of our teams. Through empowering and developing others, we forged a culture of growth, supporting the continuous development of our team members and amplifying their contributions.

Chapter 8 transported us into the realm of engaging and inspiring the organization. We mastered the art of effective communication, skillfully tailoring our messages to resonate with diverse audiences. We motivated and engaged our employees, igniting their passion and commitment to shared goals. Celebrating wins and recognizing achievements became an integral part of our leadership style, fueling a culture of celebration and fostering a sense of collective pride.

Finally, in Chapter 9, we confronted the inevitable challenges and setbacks that accompany every leadership journey. We delved into the art of dealing with difficult situations and conflict, skillfully defusing tensions and fostering harmonious resolutions. Embracing failures as invaluable opportunities for growth, we learned from our setbacks and adapted to change with resilience and perseverance. These qualities fortified us against adversity, ensuring our ability to lead with unwavering determination and grace.

As we reflect on the first 50 days of our leadership journey, we are awed by the incredible growth, resilience, and impact we have achieved. We celebrate the milestones we have crossed, the relationships we have forged, and the positive change we have ushered into our organizations. We acknowledge the valuable lessons learned from the challenges we faced, recognizing that they have served as catalysts for our personal and professional development.

Looking ahead, we stand poised at the precipice of limitless possibilities. Our leadership journey is a perpetual odyssey, an eternal quest for excellence and innovation. Let us embrace the future with unwavering passion, armed with the lessons we have learned and the wisdom we have gained. Let us continue to evolve, to inspire, and to create lasting impact.

Congratulations on completing the first 50 days of your leadership expedition. May your path be adorned with continued growth, transformative achievements, and unwavering resilience. Lead with conviction, empower those around you, and leave an indelible mark on the world through your impactful leadership.

Lessons Learned and Key Takeaways

The first 50 days of leadership have been a transformative journey, filled with profound lessons and invaluable insights. As we conclude this book, let us delve deeper into the lessons learned and explore the key takeaways that will shape our ongoing leadership expedition. These lessons and takeaways serve as the bedrock of our leadership philosophy, guiding our actions and decisions as we strive to make a lasting impact. Here, we expand upon each lesson, providing a more descriptive and comprehensive understanding of their significance:

1. **Self-awareness is the bedrock of effective leadership:** Leadership begins with self-awareness. Taking the time to understand our own strengths, weaknesses, values, and biases allows us to lead with authenticity and purpose. It enables us to make conscious choices aligned with our core principles and empowers us to leverage our strengths while seeking support and growth in areas that require improvement. Self-awareness also helps us navigate challenging situations with grace and emotional intelligence.

2. **Building relationships is essential:** Effective leadership thrives on strong relationships. Cultivating meaningful connections with key stakeholders, team members, and peers is essential for fostering trust, collaboration, and shared success. Building relationships requires active listening, empathy, and open communication. By investing time and effort in understanding the needs and aspirations of those around us, we create a supportive ecosystem that encourages collaboration, sparks innovation, and promotes a sense of belonging.

3. **The power of first impressions:** The initial days in a leadership role are crucial for establishing credibility, setting expectations, and inspiring confidence. Making a strong first impression requires a thoughtful approach. It involves demonstrating competence, clarity of vision, and an authentic leadership style. By articulating our goals, values, and expectations, we create a foundation upon which trust can flourish. First impressions lay the groundwork for building strong relationships and cultivating a culture of excellence.

4. **Embrace change and navigate it effectively:** Change is a constant companion on the leadership journey. Embracing it as an opportunity for growth and innovation is vital. Leaders must understand the need for change, craft a clear change strategy, and effectively communicate the vision behind it. By involving stakeholders in the process, gaining their buy-in, and providing support, leaders can navigate change successfully. Flexibility, adaptability, and resilience are key attributes that enable leaders to address challenges, overcome resistance, and keep the organization moving forward.

5. **Cultivate emotional intelligence:** Emotional intelligence, often regarded as the cornerstone of effective leadership, encompasses self-awareness, self-regulation, empathy, and social skills. By developing emotional intelligence, leaders can navigate complex interpersonal dynamics, build strong relationships, and foster a positive work environment. Leaders who understand and manage their emotions can inspire and motivate their teams, make informed decisions, and handle difficult situations with empathy and grace.

6. **Lead by example:** Leadership is not just about what we say but how we act. Leading by example is a powerful way to inspire and influence others. When leaders demonstrate integrity, authenticity, and a commitment to their values,

they set a standard that others aspire to. By modeling the behaviors and attitudes they expect from their teams, leaders create a culture of accountability, trust, and high performance.

7. **Communication is key:** Effective communication lies at the heart of successful leadership. Leaders must master the art of clear and concise communication, adapting their style to resonate with diverse audiences. By fostering open dialogue, actively listening, and providing timely and relevant information, leaders create a culture of transparency, collaboration, and trust. Effective communication ensures alignment, minimizes misunderstandings, and empowers teams to work towards shared goals.

8. **Foster a culture of empowerment and development:** Great leaders understand the importance of nurturing their team members' growth and potential. By providing opportunities for learning, skill development, and professional growth, leaders empower their teams to reach their full potential. Delegating responsibilities, encouraging autonomy, and creating an environment that supports innovation and creativity are essential for fostering a culture of empowerment. By investing in their team's development, leaders cultivate loyalty, engagement, and a high-performing workforce.

9. **Persevere through challenges:** Leadership is not without its share of challenges and setbacks. Great leaders exhibit resilience, perseverance, and a growth mindset when faced with obstacles. They view failures as learning opportunities and respond with agility, adaptability, and determination. By maintaining a positive attitude, staying focused on the vision, and leading with resilience, leaders inspire their teams to overcome adversity and emerge stronger.

10. **Reflect and learn from experience:** Reflection is a critical component of leadership growth. Taking the time to pause, introspect, and learn from both successes and failures allows leaders to refine their approach, expand their perspectives, and continuously improve. Reflection enables leaders to recognize patterns, identify areas for growth, and make informed decisions based on past experiences. By embracing a culture of continuous learning and self-reflection, leaders can stay ahead of the curve and navigate future challenges with wisdom and insight.

These lessons and key takeaways encapsulate the essence of leading with impact in the first 50 days and beyond. They serve as guiding principles, shaping our mindset, behaviors, and actions as we embark on our ongoing leadership journey. By embracing these lessons, adapting them to our unique context, and consistently applying them, we can cultivate impactful leadership that leaves a lasting legacy. Let us carry these lessons in our hearts and minds, and may they continue to inspire and guide us on our path to creating positive change.

Looking Ahead: Sustaining Impactful Leadership

As we reflect on the first 50 days of our leadership journey, we are filled with a sense of accomplishment and growth. The foundations we have laid, the relationships we have built, and the challenges we have overcome have positioned us for long-term success. However, sustaining impactful leadership requires a relentless pursuit of growth, learning, and adaptation. Looking ahead, let us explore the key strategies and principles that will guide us in sustaining our impact as leaders, while also igniting a sense of excitement and engagement:

1. **Embrace a Growth Mindset:** Leaders who embrace a growth mindset understand that their abilities and skills can be developed through dedication, effort, and continuous learning. They see challenges as opportunities for growth, setbacks as stepping stones to success, and failures as valuable lessons. By adopting a growth mindset, we open ourselves up to new possibilities, push past our limitations, and inspire others to do the same. Remember, it is not about being perfect; it is about the willingness to learn, improve, and evolve.

2. **Cultivate a Culture of Learning:** Sustaining impactful leadership requires creating a culture where learning is not just encouraged but celebrated. Foster an environment where curiosity is nurtured, and intellectual curiosity is rewarded. Provide resources, training programs, and mentorship opportunities to support ongoing development. Encourage your team members to explore new ideas, experiment with innovative approaches, and share their knowledge with others. By making learning a priority, you create a dynamic

organization that adapts quickly to change and stays ahead of the competition.

3. **Nurture Leadership Succession:** As impactful leaders, we have a responsibility to cultivate the next generation of leaders. Identify and nurture high-potential individuals within your organization, invest in their development, and provide them with opportunities to stretch their abilities. Create mentorship programs, offer leadership training, and delegate responsibilities to help them build the skills and confidence needed for future leadership roles. By actively grooming successors, you ensure the continuity of impactful leadership and leave a lasting legacy.

4. **Stay Agile and Adaptive:** The business landscape is in a constant state of flux, and sustaining impactful leadership requires agility and adaptability. Stay informed about industry trends, technological advancements, and emerging market shifts. Embrace a proactive approach to change by regularly assessing the effectiveness of your strategies and adjusting them as needed. Encourage a culture of innovation, where new ideas are welcomed, and calculated risks are encouraged. By staying agile and adaptive, you position yourself and your organization for continued success in a rapidly changing world.

5. **Foster Collaboration and Engagement:** Sustaining impactful leadership is not a solo endeavor. It requires fostering a culture of collaboration and engagement within your organization. Break down silos and encourage cross-functional collaboration by creating opportunities for teams to work together on shared projects and initiatives. Foster a sense of belonging by promoting inclusivity, diversity, and respect for differing perspectives. Actively seek input from your team members, value their contributions, and empower them to make decisions. By creating a collaborative and engaged environment, you harness the collective intelligence

and creativity of your team, driving sustained innovation and growth.

6. **Lead with Purpose:** Purpose-driven leadership is a catalyst for sustained impact. Clarify your leadership purpose and ensure it aligns with the values and goals of your organization. Communicate your purpose effectively to inspire and motivate your team members. Let your actions speak louder than words by consistently demonstrating your commitment to your purpose through your decisions and behaviors. When you lead with purpose, you create a sense of meaning, direction, and unity that fuels the long-term success of your organization.

7. **Seek Feedback and Foster Growth:** Sustaining impactful leadership requires a willingness to seek feedback and embrace opportunities for growth. Actively seek input from your team members, peers, mentors, and other stakeholders. Be open to different perspectives, and use feedback as a springboard for self-reflection and improvement. Create a safe and supportive environment where constructive feedback is valued and celebrated. Encourage continuous learning and development by providing resources, coaching, and mentorship to support the growth of both yourself and your team members.

8. **Balance Well-being and Performance:** Sustaining impactful leadership is not solely about driving performance; it is also about caring for the well-being of yourself and your team members. Recognize that sustainable success requires a balance between achieving goals and maintaining physical, mental, and emotional well-being. Lead by example by prioritizing self-care, setting boundaries, and promoting work-life integration. Encourage your team members to prioritize their well-being, provide support when needed, and create a culture that values work-life balance. When individuals are healthy and fulfilled, they are more engaged,

productive, and resilient, driving sustained success for the entire organization.

Looking ahead, our leadership journey is an adventure filled with endless possibilities, challenges, and opportunities for growth. By embracing a growth mindset, cultivating a culture of learning, nurturing leadership succession, staying agile and adaptive, fostering collaboration and engagement, leading with purpose, seeking feedback and fostering growth, and balancing well-being and performance, we can sustain our impact as leaders and create a legacy that transcends time. Let us embark on this journey with passion, courage, and an unwavering commitment to excellence. The path ahead may be challenging, but with our collective efforts, we can shape a brighter future for ourselves, our teams, and our organizations.

About the Author

Mr. Raul Dominguez is a highly regarded leader and expert in organizational psychology. With a Master's degree in Industrial-Organizational Psychology, he has dedicated his career to empowering individuals and organizations to achieve their full potential. Mr. Dominguez's extensive experience in leadership development, change management, and employee engagement has made him a sought-after speaker and consultant. His book, "Leading with Impact: The First 50 Days," draws upon his expertise to provide practical strategies and real-world examples for aspiring and current leaders. With a passion for inspiring others and a deep understanding of effective leadership practices, Mr. Dominguez continues to make a profound impact on individuals and organizations around the world.

www.ingramcontent.com/pod-product-compliance
Lightning Source LLC
Chambersburg PA
CBHW031549210526
45464CB00003B/1226